ARTFOLDS

.....................................

This book belongs to

.....................................

Folded by

D1611728

Color Editions No. 1

# HEART

*featuring*
Random Acts of Caring

by Stephanie Schwartz

Studio Fun Books
White Plains, New York • Montréal, Québec • Bath, United Kingdom

ArtFolds™
Color Editions No. 1
Heart

ArtFolds is a patent-pending process for folding pages based on a set
of unique printed marks to create a sculpture out of a bound book.

To learn more about ArtFolds, visit artfolds.com

Customized and/or prefolded ArtFolds are available. To explore
options and pricing, email specialorder@artfolds.com.

To discover the wide range of products available from
Studio Fun International, visit studiofun.com

Address any comments about ArtFolds to:
Publisher
Studio Fun Books
44 South Broadway, 7th floor
White Plains, NY 10601

Or send an email to publisher@artfolds.com.

Printed in China
Conforms to ASTM F963

1 3 5 7 9 10 8 6 4 2 LPP/04/14
ISBN 978-0-7944-3220-1

# About ArtFolds

THE BOOK YOU HOLD in your hands is more than just a book. It's an ArtFolds! Inside are simple instructions that will show you how to fold the pages to transform this book into a beautiful heart-shaped sculpture. No special skill is required; all you'll do is carefully fold the corners of marked book pages, based on the folding lines provided. When complete, you'll have created a long-lasting work of art. It's fun and easy, and can be completed in just one evening!

To add to the experience, each ArtFolds contains compelling reading content. In this edition, you'll discover lots of simple but clever ways to show your love to family, friends, coworkers, or classmates.

Each ArtFolds edition is designed by an established, professional book sculptor whose works are routinely displayed and sold in art galleries, museum shops, and online crafts and art stores. ArtFolds celebrates this community of artists and encourages you to support this expanding art form by seeking out their work and sharing their unique designs and creations with others.

To learn more about ArtFolds, visit **artfolds.com**. There you'll find details of all ArtFolds editions, instructional videos, and much more.

# The ArtFolds Portfolio

## Color Editions

These smaller ArtFolds™ editions use a range of colors printed on each page to make each sculpture a multi-colored work of art. Titles now or soon available include:

Edition 1: Heart
Edition 2: Mickey Mouse
Edition 3: Christmas Tree
Edition 4: MOM
Edition 5: Flower

## Classic Editions

These larger ArtFolds™ editions include the full text of a classic book; when folded, book text appears along the edges, creating a piece of art that celebrates the dignity and beauty of a printed book. Titles now or soon available include:

Edition 1: LOVE
Edition 2: Snowflake
Edition 3: JOY
Edition 4: READ
Edition 5: Sun

To see the full range of ArtFolds editions, visit **artfolds.com.**

# About the Designer

The sculpture design in this edition was created exclusively for ArtFolds by Luciana Frigerio. Based in Vermont, Luciana has been making photographs, objects, book sculptures, and artistic mischief for over 30 years. Her work has been exhibited in galleries and museums around the world. Luciana's artwork can be found at: lucianafrigerio.com, and her unique, customized book sculptures can be found in her shop on the online crafts market Etsy at: etsy.com/shop/LucianaFrigerio.

# Instructions

Creating your ArtFolds Color Editions book sculpture is easy! Just follow these simple instructions and guidelines:

1. Always fold right-hand pages.

2. Always fold toward you.

1, 2

3. All folding pages require two folds: The top corner will fold down, and the bottom corner will fold up.

4. Grasp the top right corner of the page, and fold until the side of the page aligns exactly with the TOP of the horizontal color bar.

4

5. Grasp the bottom right corner of the page, and fold upward until the side of the page aligns exactly with the BOTTOM of the horizontal color bar.

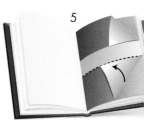

5

6. Carefully run your finger across the folds to make sure they are straight, crisp, and accurate.

7. Continue on to the next page and repeat until your ArtFolds book sculpture is complete!

## Extra advice

- We recommend washing and then thoroughly drying your hands prior to folding.

- Some folders prefer using a tool to help make fold lines straight and sharp. Bone folders, metal rulers, popsicle sticks, or any other firm, straight tool will work.

- Some folders prefer to rotate their book sideways to make folding easier.

- Remember: The more accurate you are with each fold, the more accurate your completed book sculpture will be!

Folding begins after page 21 and continues for the next 90 right-hand pages.

For more folding instructions and videos, visit **artfolds.com**

*Featuring*

# RANDOM ACTS OF CARING

*Simple Ways to Show Friends and Family How Much You Care*

Pick up a pretty flower,
leaf, or stone and
**give it to someone
special.**

**Play together—**
tennis or backgammon,
it doesn't matter as long
as you both have fun.

Leave a small
**bag of cookies**
in your mailbox
for the mail carrier,
just because it's
Thursday.

Make your
**compliments
as sincere**
as your criticism.

Be the first one
**to apologize**
after a fight.

Tell someone,
**"I'm proud
of you."**

Celebrate your birthday
by performing one
**act of caring**
for every year of
your life.

# Hold the door open
for the person
behind you.

Give a
**big, big hug**
right before dinner.

# Be on time.
## Always.

Spend
**one-on-one**
time with friends and
family members.

Find a good joke,
and **share it** with
your pals.

**Donate clothes,**
toys, and books to
organizations that share
them with people who
need them.

Ask people about
their day and
**really listen
to the answers.**

Greet people
with a
**big smile**
and a
**warm hello.**

Be generous with
your time—
**it's the best
gift of all.**

**Serve breakfast in bed,**
and not just on Sundays!

# Decorate the living room
## with balloons.

Tell the story of
**the first time
you met.**

Give at least three
**heart-felt
compliments**
each day.

**Share some
hot cocoa**
on a rainy
Sunday afternoon.

**Plant a garden together.**
Then be sure to tend to it together.

**Clear your schedules** and go for a walk in the park on a beautiful day.

♡

**Stay in on
Saturday night
together,**
and watch your
favorite movie.

**Do the chores—**
all of them, not just
your own—without
being asked.

Turn off the phone,
the television, and the
computer, and
**give someone
your full
attention.**

# Memorize
# a poem

to recite to
someone you
care for.

Get to know a
resident of a nearby
nursing home, and
**visit often.**

# Don't compare people with others—

## we're all special in our own ways.

**Just say "yes" sometimes—**
to ice cream for breakfast or cereal for dinner, to ditching the chores and having an adventure instead....

## Say
## "I love you"
at least once
every day.